# Resin Jewellery

# Resin Jewelry

## KATHIE MURPHY

Krause Publications

*For Jonathan and Naomi*

Acknowledgements and thanks to all the makers whose work is included in this book. Thanks also to Michelle Tiernan, Dermot Murphy, William Teakle, Colin Williamson, Nick Orsborne, Libby Slater, Adele Tipler, The Natural History Museum, Thomas Gentille, Alan Durrant, Macer Hall and not forgetting Christine, my mother and librarian.

First published in Great Britain 2002
A & C Black Publishers Ltd
37 Soho Square, London W1D 3QZ
www.acblack.com

Copyright © 2002 Kathie Murphy

ISBN 0-7136-5275-6

Published simultaneously in the USA by Krause Publications, Iola, Wis.

ISBN 0-87349-619-1

Library of Congress Catalog No. 2002110349

Kathie Murphy has asserted her right under the Copyright, Design and Patents Act, 1988, to be identified as the author of this work

A CIP catalog record for this book is available from the British Linrary and the US Library of Congress

*Front cover illustration*: Earrings, resin and rubber, by Kathie Murphy, 1995. Photo by K.S. Muphy.
*Back cover illustrations*: (Top) Pearl and resin brooch, by Kathie Murphy, 2001. Photo by K.S. Murphy. (Bottom) Necklace, resin and meta foil, by Kathie Murphy, 1994. Photo K.S. Murphy
*Frontispiece*: Bangle, resin, by Cara Croninger. Photo by Hugh Ball.
Design by Keith & Clair Watson
Cover design by Dorothy Moir

Disclaimer: Information given in this book is to the author's best knowledge and every effort has been made to ensure accuracy and safety but neither the author not publisher can be held responsible for any resulting injury, damage or loss to either persons or property. Any further information which will assist in updating of any future editions would be gratefully received. Read right through this book before commencing work in resin. Follow all health and safety guidelines and, where necessary, obtain health and safety information from the suppliers

Printed and bound in Singapore by Tien Wah Press

A & C Black uses paper produced with elemental chlorine-free pulp, harvested from managed sustainable sources

# CONTENTS

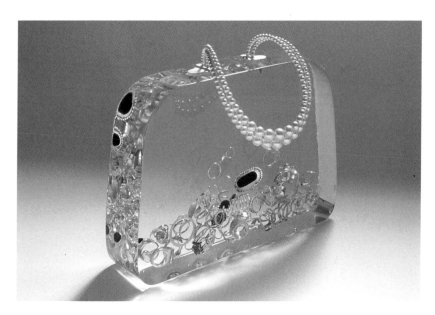

**Ted Noten**
*Ageeths Bridesgroam,* acrylic resin.
Photo by Matthijs Muller.

# INTRODUCTION

Over the last seven years of working in polyester resin I have had difficulty in finding any books on the subject of working in resin on a craft scale. Most of the books date from the 1970s and are either too chemical or too basic. A number of other makers and students have also found this to be the case and I have received telephone calls and letters asking me for technical advice. Not always the easiest thing to do over the telephone! Scare stories on the dangers of the material and the lack of information available to those who are interested in working in resins made me accept the offer to write this book.

I first started to use resin at college as a binder in a composite material. From this an interest in resin itself developed. It is a versatile material that can be coloured easily and also made to be transparent or transluscent as well as textured. From the raw material, a liquid, it was possible to be innovative and create ones own solid plastic. Resin was not like other plastics I had worked in, it was not cold to the touch and with brittle sharp edges. The tactile element lent itself well as a material from which to make jewellery.

Whether working in resin in small or larger quantities it does not have to be dangerous. A few simple health and safety measures can be taken; wearing an organic vapours mask, barrier cream and working in a well ventilated area and general common sense with regard to cleaning up and extracting any dust created. This book will guide those who are not familiar with the material and aid those who have some experience of the material. Building up information about a material means that a familiarity with its problems and advantages will result in the ability to control the results of experimentation and use them to effect in jewellery designs.

**Malcolm Chance (England)**
Bangles, acrylic and resin.
Photo Daniel Welles.

# CHAPTER ONE

# A Brief History of Plastic

Developing a knowledge of the history of the material in which you undertake to work furthers the understanding of its aesthetic quality and its importance in relation to our culture and environment.

Resin, as part of the plastics family, shares in the misfortune of being generally regarded as cheap, disposable and without merit; inferior to natural materials. How did plastic get this reputation and is it likely to change?

A plastic is a material that can be moulded into useful shapes through heat and sometimes pressure. There are many different types of plastic ranging from the natural to the man-made. All are made from organic polymers. A polymer is a long chain of many thousands of large molecules or monomers. A monomer is made up of smaller molecules, carbon atoms, with the ability to form links with other molecules. These monomers then join up to form a long chain. The process by which they link up to form long chains is called polymerisation.

Polymers can occur naturally in protein and cellulose. Natural plastics exist such as horn, shellac, amber and tortoiseshell. Semi-synthetic plastics are those made by modifying natural polymers, cellulose or caesin, a milk protein with other chemicals. Synthetic plastics are derived from polymers made from hydrocarbons that have been extracted from crude oil, there are many hundreds of different kinds of synthetic plastic.

Plastics fall into two catagories, thermoplastics and thermosetting plastics. Thermoplastics are those which soften on heating and are solid when cold. Natural thermoplastics are glass, ice and wax. Plastics that fall into this category can be reheated and formed, they are able to do this as the long polymer chains do not have any bonds between them and move relative to each other when heated. In order to form them into objects some form of heat and pressure is required. Examples of these plastics are acrylic, polythene and cellulose acetate.

Thermosetting plastics undergo a single change through heat and sometimes pressure to form a solid. This is explained by the fact that during this process the long chains of polymers form crosslinks or bonds. Once these are formed it is not possible to change the shape of the plastic as the bonds do not allow the polymer chains to move, making them less flexible. Most resins such as epoxy, polyurethane and polyester

**Cicada (England)**
Brooches, resin, 1974.
Photo courtesy Brighton University.

**Susanna Heron (England)**
Bracelet, resin and silver, 1971.
Photo Ray Carpenter.

are thermosetting. The liquid plastic is turned to a solid by the addition of a catalyst or hardner and this is the crosslinking agent. Polyurethanes and polyesters are versatile polymers, they can be both thermoplastic; fibres or thermosetting; foams and resins.

Plastics have been used for many hundreds of years to make useful and decorative objects. Natural plastics such as horn and tortoiseshell were moulded through heat and pressure into buckles and boxes, as well as other sorts of container. Rather than individually crafting products, costs could be reduced and many of the same item reproduced. An early thermosetting plastic such as Bois Durci patented in 1855 was made from the albumen

11

**Betty Heald (USA)**
Wrist form, resin and silver, 1990.
Photo Betty Heald.

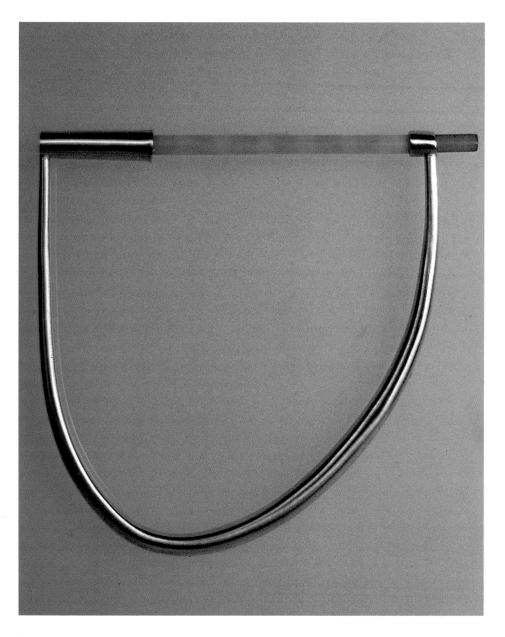

they became sticky, smelly or brittle after a short time.

Technical advances in the 1960s meant it was a boom time for the plastics industry. It was seen as the material of the future and used by designers in making futuristic clothing, jewellery and furniture. The constant demand for new ideas and goods was easily met by plastics' rapid production methods. The consumer accelerated a disposable world.

The sculptors of the 1960s and 1970s also saw the possibilities of plastic. Artists such as Duane Hanson and Claus Oldenberg used GRP to realise large colourful sculptures which were lightweight and robust. Although, as the range of plastics increased, they moved on to use other materials in their work. This could have been because the sculptors were not always very accurate when mixing their polyester resin and this resulted in some of the sculptures deteriorating rapidly outdoors.

The energy crisis in the 1970s was another disastrous moment in the history of plastics. The huge increase in the price of oil and the global recession meant the rapid expansion of the plastics industry had to be stopped. Coupled with a reaction to the 'Synthetic Sixties' and environmental concerns about the toxicity of plastics, plastic once again became a derogatory word.

Plastics' reputation as an inexpensive material made it the perfect medium for the 'New Jewellery' of the 1970s. A reaction by artist jewellers to ostentatious and expensive jewellery resulted in an increased use of non-precious materials. It also introduced bright colour to jewellery. Susanna Heron was one such pioneer and first used resin in 1971, inlaying it in silver. She moved into acrylics and other materials as her ideas expanded. Unlike some of the sculptures from this time, her bangles in resin do not appear to have suffered any deterioration.

Plastics continued to interest designers and makers in the 1980s. In Italy and Germany the use of plastic in products did not bring about the same disdainful reaction by consumers and industrial designers used it for household goods and furniture to great acclaim. Consumers in Britain began to come around to plastic products as the fashion for 'designer' items increased.

The production methods and properties of plastics have vastly improved over the last fifteen years. Plastics are accepted for what they are now and are also highly sophisticated fakers: able to simulate an enormous number of other natural materials – wood, plants, silks and furs. They have replaced metals in many areas of our lives and are so strong and heat resistant today, that a plastic tank is used by the Army.

Where plastics continue to receive little acclaim is studio jewellery. Because plastic products tend to be

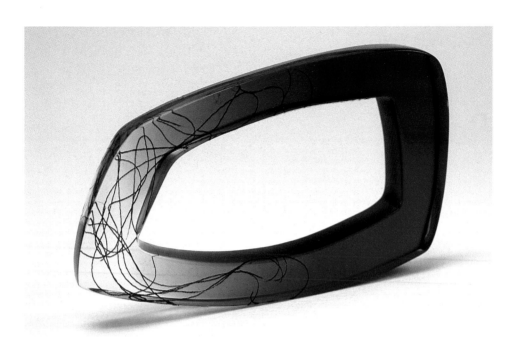

**Kathie Murphy (England)**
Bangle, resin and thread, 1999.
Photo K.S. Murphy.

# Types of Resin

There are many different types of
casting resin available, each having
their own properties and specific
applications. This book deals with
those that are suitable for use in
jewellery and most readily available
over the counter in small quantities.
Polyester resin is the resin most
commonly used as an example in
this book but there are a few
examples of Polyurethane resin and
epoxy resin.

Resin is a thermosetting plastic. It
comes as a liquid which by the
addition of a hardener or catalyst
undergoes a non-reversible
exothermic reaction to become a
solid. Polyester resin would set
without a catalyst over a period of
months. To speed up the reaction an
activator or accelerator is added. **Try
to always use a pre-activated resin,
as catalyst and activator when
mixed directly together can react
violently.** During the reaction, the
resin undergoes a chemical change
which is polymerisation or curing.
Resin has an advantage over other
thermosetting plastics in that it is
possible to mould it at low pressure
without the use of external heat.

The polymerisation of the resin
produces a gradual build up of heat
which can reach a peak of around
150°C (302°F), an exothermic

reaction. Too much heat can set up stresses in the resin, leading to cracking or crazing. To avoid this do not use insulated moulds, or aid the dispersal of heat by cooling the mould by standing it in a bath of cold water. Adding less catalyst can help to reduce the heat produced and this is particularly necessary in large castings. The exotherm can also affect the shrinkage of the resin, the lower the exotherm the less the shrinkage rate.

Resin changes through polymerisation from a liquid to a gel (jelly like) in around 25 minutes, after 2-3 hours it sets to a solid and becomes completely hard or fully cured after 24 hours to a week.

There are several types of resin that can be used in jewellery. There will be a resin more suitable for a certain application than another. They differ in viscosity as well as in appearance and some resins are better suited to large castings and

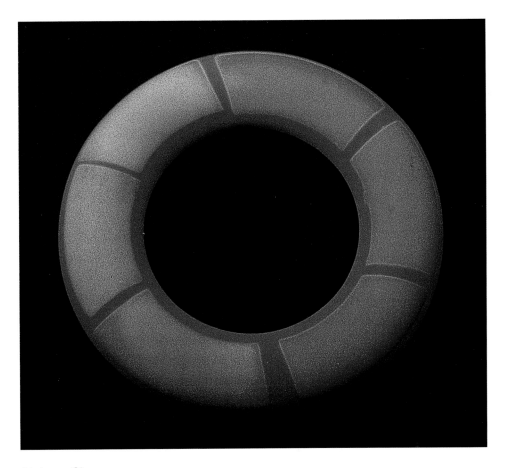

**Malcom Chance**
Bangle, resin and acrylic.
Photo M. Chance.

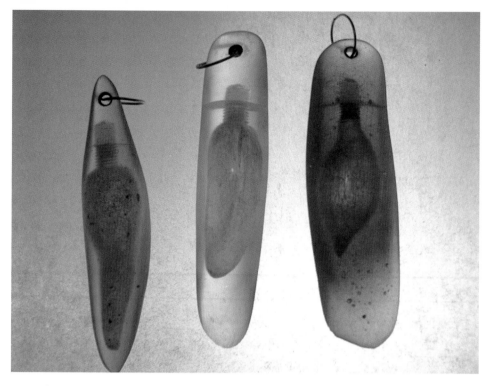

**Kate Groombridge (England)**
Pendant, resin.
Photo K. Groombridge.

will not set in thin sections or small amounts. Resins tend to vary from supplier to supplier too, even though they sound similar in description. The majority of resins available in small quantities are pre-activated or pre-accelerated (PA).

## Clear casting or embedding resin

This is a water-clear resin that is most often used for entrapping flora and fauna specimens and for the addition of translucent colour pastes. It is slightly more expensive than other resins. Clear casting resin is a very thin pourable resin, (low viscosity) and is ideal where delicate flowers or objects with recesses need to be encapsulated in resin. It has a tendency to remain tacky on any exposed surfaces. This allows the resin to be built up in layers, giving greater adherance from one new layer to another.

There are differences within the types of clear casting resin. Some have a tendency to yellow over time but this can be due to inaccurate measuring of catalyst, most likely that too much catalyst has been added. There is a clear casting resin available which has been modified with acrylic (methyl mathacrylate) and this remains clear with no short-term appearance of discolouring.

The latter resin also has the same refractive index as glass when it is fully cured. Some can be cast into flexible moulds and others can only be cast into rigid moulds as the flexible materials inhibit the curing of the resin and the result is a sticky mess.

## Casting and general purpose resin

These resins vary greatly in appearance but all are slightly tinted or cloudy but unpigmented. They can be coloured using resin pastes or filled with other materials such as marble powder, calcium carbonate, slate powder, and sintered metals. Glass powder or fibres can be added to reinforce the resin where larger castings are required. The volume of filler to resin can vary from a 50:50 proportion to 70:30 by weight. The viscosity of the resins differ from a low viscosity, easily cast into moulds to a more thixotropic, which can be layed up over fibre glass matting and rovings. They can be cast into flexible and rigid moulds.

## Gelcoat Resin

A thixotropic resin with high viscosity, used where there are vertical surfaces or it is required not to run off. The word gelcoat also means the thin, smooth outer layer of unreinforced resin applied to hide the visible pattern of reinforcing material in layers beneath. The gelcoat also protects the glassfibre from attack by moisture. It is unpigmented and can be coloured using resin pastes. There is a company who supply a water clear gelcoat resin. A thixotropic additive can be used with other resins to create a gelcoat. There are additives such as Cabosil that when added to

23

**Dawn Gulyas**
Brooch, resin, rubber and steel, 1999.
Photo credit Joel Degen.

## Jesmonite

A non-toxic resin that is safer to use than the previously mentioned resins. Jesmonite is a polymerised acrylic in water. The catalyst added removes the water allowing it to set. As it is water based it can be thinned using water, or with the addition of a thixotropic agent becomes paste like. It is more expensive but does not require as many safety precautions as other resins and the tools can be cleaned in water. Totally opaque and chalky in appearance, the range of colours is not as great as those of polyester resin. Realistic stone effects can be achieved with it and it picks up minute detail from moulds. Jesmonite expands by 0.1% to fit the mould. It is better when it has been reinforced with matting or fibre and then forms an immensely strong material which increases in tensile strength with age. Very thin castings are possible where the Jesmonite is reinforced, and it can be used as an adhesive for itself. There is a Jesmonite available which can be carved easily and could then be used as a master for a silicone rubber mould. Being non-toxic, it has attracted conservators at the British Museum and the artist Rachel Whiteread. Most suitable for use in open moulds.

# Health and Safety

An important aspect of working in resin is to carefully read and take note of the health and safety issues and guidelines. All suppliers of resin products in the UK are obliged under The Control of Substances Hazardous to Health Regulations 1988 (COSHH) to give information on their safe use and handling. It is advisable that you are aware of the potential hazards that exist with this material before starting work with it. As with other craft materials, there are a few simple rules in the handling and use of resins that should be adhered to in order to enjoy the experience of working in the material. The potential hazards that exist are to the skin, eyes and respiratory system and as a fire and explosion hazard.

It is very easy to be complacent about simple precautions that can be taken to protect ones health. Even for five minutes of working time in resin it is worth putting on a face mask, or using barrier cream and gloves to prevent skin irritations.

## Skin

Polyester resin may cause irritation to the skin and polyurethane and epoxy resins can cause dermatitis. It is advisable to use a barrier cream to protect exposed areas of the skin as well as using PVC or polythene disposable gloves. The resin is a very sticky liquid and not easily cleaned off skin. Should you get any on you do not use solvents, such as acetone to remove the resin, as it is a strong de-greaser and can result in harmful effects to the body. Wash off any resin using a cleansing cream and plenty of water.

Avoid getting catalyst on the skin, should this occur then wash off thoroughly with water and apply a lanolin based ointment afterwards.

## Eyes

You only have one pair. They are at risk from dust particles and in particular the organic liquid catalyst. Wear goggles to protect your eyes when using machinery. Irrigate thoroughly with water for ten minutes should your eyes get resin or catalyst in them. Seek medical attention.

HIGHLY FLAMMABLE
Substance, especially its vapour, that will cause violent explosive fire if used near naked flame or electrical equipment.

CORROSIVE
Severe or life threatning substance which causes burning, or defoliation or blistering to skin and internal tissue, and damage to eyes.

IRRITANT
Substance that has undramatic effect, but can cause serious injury to eyes, skin and respiratory tissue with long exposure.

HARMFUL
Substance can cause non life threatening but severe injury via ingestion, inhalation or absorption through the skin.

OXIDISING
Oxidising substances can cause fire in contact with combustible material, without the introduction of a naked flame or spark.

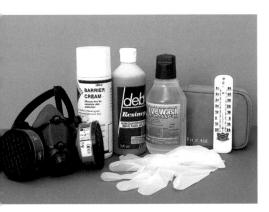

Health and safety products from left to right: organic vapours mask, barrier cream, hand cleaner, eye wash, first aid, themometer (room temperature) and PVC gloves.
Photo William Teakle.

## Respiratory

Polyester resin has a strong odour and work produced in the material results in styrene fumes being released in to the air. Polyurethane resin is odourless but the fumes are more harmful than resin. It is easy to be complacent as there is not a smell to remind you to wear a mask.

**With all resins, good ventilation and the use of a filtered face mask is always required.**

It is strongly suggested that work is not carried out in a domestic environment. Where only small quantities of resin are being used at a time (25g-250g) then a workroom where the windows and door can be opened to allow a circulation of air will be sufficient to prevent the high concentration of harmful fumes.

If it is not possible to work in a fume cabinet then to ensure a circulation of air it is advisable to use some form of extraction and/or a machine which will blow fresh air into the work area. Any extraction used should be placed at ground level as resin fumes are heavier than air and therefore sink to the floor. During hot weather the evaporation rate increases and ventilation should be increased.

More harmful to your health is the dust as this cannot be broken down by the body. **Always wear a dust mask**, the better the mask the greater the protection. An industrial vacuum cleaner is invaluable for removing dust particles.

**Do not smoke when using these materials.**

## Storage of resin products

All resins should be stored in cool, dry conditions and at temperatures no higher than 20°C (67°F). The lower the storage temperature the longer the shelf life of the resin but it is advisable to keep them for no longer than three months. Any temperature above 20°C (67°F) will considerably shorten the shelf life of the resin. Resin also has a flash point of less than 32°C (89°F), which means? **A fire hazard.** Mark the container with the date of delivery so there is no confusion and only buy as much as you need. Catalyst (organic peroxide) and activator (cobalt octoate or napthanate) should be stored in seperate, preferably metal cabinets. **Catalyst**

28

and activator should never be mixed directly, this would result in a violent explosion. Wherever possible use pre-activated resin.

Catalysts and hardeners should be stored in the dark away from flammable materials and not placed in the sun or near a heat source. It is liable to spontaneous combustion if it gets hot. **A fire hazard.** Sunlight and time will also diminsh it strength.

Acetone is **highly flammable** with a flash point below 0°C and should be clearly marked. Store in a metal cupboard if possible well away from any naked flames and beware of electrical sparks.

## *Disposal*

Any disposal of large quantities of resin material should be carried out by a specialist. After working in resin there may be small quantites of catalysed resin left over, this can be left in the mixing container to cure. Any amount over 10mm ($^3/_8$ in.) in depth in the bottom of the container should be spread out or cooled down to prevent a build-up of heat as the temperature of curing resin can rise to 150°C and disposed of once the heat has subsided completely. This is particularly important where there might be other inflammable material in the waste bin that the resin may come into contact with. Spillages of resin should be covered with sand and removed to an open area. Smaller spillages can be cleared up with rags or paper and burned in a controlled area as soon as possible. Do not use the same rags or paper to mop up different materials, such as activator and catalyst. It could lead to a violent reaction. Rags and paper that have been in contact with resins and other liquids should be placed in a container that can be closed and regularly disposed of. **Do not pour resins and other chemicals down the sink.**

**Karen Robertson (Scotland)**
Ring, resin and magnets, 2001.
Photo K. Robertson.

29

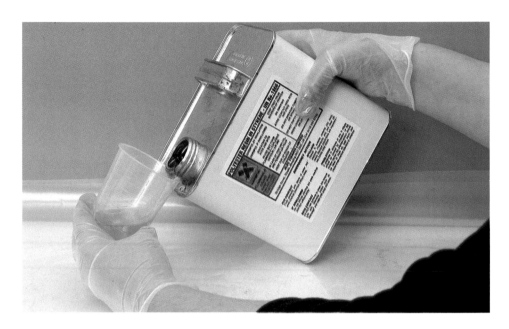

Correct method for pouring resin.
Photo William Teakle.

adhere to or melt PVC or polythene, containers made from these materials can also be used. Do not use a polystyrene cup as the resin will dissolve it.

The measuring container should be about two thirds full and with a small surface area rather than a wide, shallow container with a greater surface area. The latter is more likely to pull air into the resin while mixing. It is important not to get air into the resin. Creating bubbles may result in a poor surface once the resin is poured into the mould. You may want a textured effect in the resin using bubbles but it is not that easy to control and would require some experimen-tation. To minimise the amount of air in the resin, it should be poured and

mixed carefully. The less thixotropic resins tend to de-gas by themselves, this means any bubbles in the resin will rise to the surface and disappear without having to tease them out.

# Measure

You should always read the manufacturer's directions first. Depending on the type of resin being used there are different methods of mixing resin, so check first.

# Calculating the quantity required

In order not to waste resin or suddenly run out when a mould is half full, it is useful to know how much you will need *before* starting to pour it out.

Water inhibits the curing of resin so the mould would have to be absolutely dry before pouring in the resin. This would definitely not work for polyurethane resins, as they hate moisture.

If you do not need to be so precise about how much resin you are going

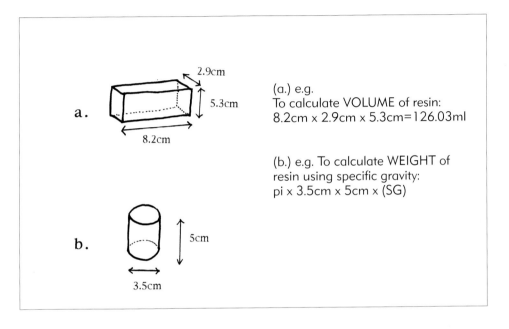

**a.** 2.9cm, 5.3cm, 8.2cm

(a.) e.g.
To calculate VOLUME of resin:
8.2cm x 2.9cm x 5.3cm=126.03ml

(b.) e.g. To calculate WEIGHT of resin using specific gravity:
pi x 3.5cm x 5cm x (SG)

**b.** 5cm, 3.5cm

If your mould is a simple shape it is possible to calculate the volume of the cavity. The cubic area can be found by multiplying base area x height or thickness of the mould. The volume of a cylinder is found using the formula (pi) 3.14 x diameter x height.

Although far from the best method, it is possible to work out the quantity of resin needed for a mould by filling the mould with water and then pouring it into a measuring cup to give you a reading.

to need, then mix in small quantities, around 50g-100g at a time and either leave what you do not use in the cup to cure or have some other moulds to hand, into which you can pour the excess.

## Polyester resin

All polyester resins need the addition of liquid catalyst, methyl etyl ketone peroxide (MEKP). The quantity of catalyst required varies depending on the size of casting to be carried out, it can be as little as 0.3% for very large castings (1kg+) to 2% on small castings (100g or less). Most jewellery-sized castings require around 2%. **To avoid overheating in larger castings add less catalyst.**

There are two basic ways of calculating the ratio of resin to catalyst. It can either be done by weight or by volume. The following tables give an idea of resin to catalyst measurements. In researching this book the number of drops per 1g/1ml

of catalyst varied so I have given a ballpark figure for drops in the section on calculating measurements by volume as this method is less accurate anyway. The discolouration of resins can occur where the measurement of catalyst has been inaccurate.

If you are using a pre-filled resin, the amount of catalyst is based on the weight of the resin content only. Check the percentage of filler.

| BY WEIGHT USING SCALES AND MEASURING DISPENSER | |
|---|---|
| RESIN | catalyst@2% (1ml of catalyst =1g) |
| 25g   (0.88oz) | 0.5ml |
| 50g   (1.76oz) | 1ml |
| 100g  (3.53oz) | 2ml |
| 250g  (8.82oz) | 5ml |

Calculating quantity of resin by weight, the syringe is for measuring the catalyst.
Photo William Teakle.

34

Remember to zero your scales with the mixing pot on it before weighing.

A simple calculation to work out the weight of the resin (where no scales are available) is to measure in a calibrated polypropylene cup, usually marked off in 50ml calibrations and multiply by specific gravity. Specific gravity (SG) means that 1ml (1cc) of a liquid weighs the SG number in grams.

The specific gravity of resin is between 1.1 and 1.15. An example of a calculation is set out below, where the SG is set at 1.12.

## NO SCALES – USING SPECIFIC GRAVITY

50ml of resin is (50 x 1.12)g=56g

100ml of resin is (100 x 1.12)g=112g        100g of resin is 89ml

to measure the catalyst at 2%        2% of 112g=2.24g or 2.24 ml

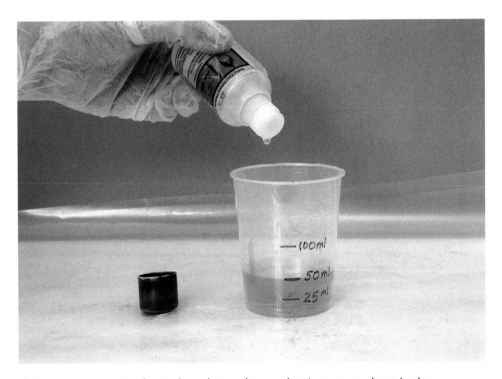

Calculating quantity of resin by volume, the catalyst is measured out in drops.
Photo William Teakle.

## BY VOLUME USING A CALIBRATED CUP AND CATALYST BY DROPS

| RESIN | catalyst@2% |
|-------|-------------|
| 25ml | 11-17 drops |
| 50ml | 22-33 drops |
| 100ml | 45-66 drops |
| 250ml | 100-150 drops |

Most of the time the small quantities of resin required for jewellery need not be quite so accurately calculated. The method given in the table above is less messy and quicker. Catalyst dispensers are liable to fall over, spilling any liquid they might contain in the measuring cylinder, which is a possible hazard of contamination and fire. A safer method is to use the small bottles of catalyst which allow the bottle to be used a bit like a pipette and the gentle squeezing of the bottle will dispense the catalyst in drops.

## Polyurethane Resin

Check the supplier's instuctions or those on the front of the package. Usually mixed by weight or volume ratio. There are many types of polyurethane available, it is possible to obtain cured samples from the supplier.

## Epoxy resin

Follow the instuctions given on the container. Again usually mixed by weight or volume ratio. Resin (part A) is usually combined with hardener (part B) in a 2:1 ratio.

## Jesmonite

The base of the Jesmonite comes as a powder and the 'catalyst' as a liquid. They are measured by weight at a ratio of 2:1 (powder: liquid).

# Mixing

Before beginning to mix your resin, have your mould(s) ready and have planned what you are going to do with the resin. Most suppliers supply a disposable wooden lollipop type stick or spatula for stirring the resin. A stirring implement that is least likely to disturb the surface of the resin is best, where a  lollipop

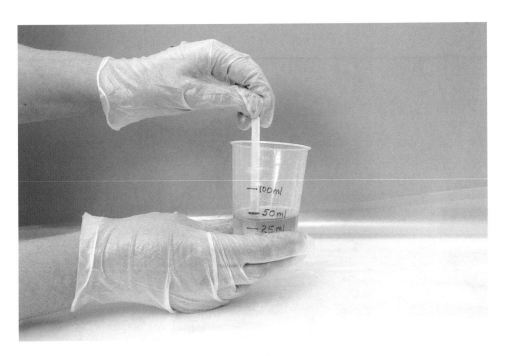

Stir the resin carefully, avoid pulling air into the mixture.
Photo William Teakle.

stick is not available. With polyurethane resin, the wooden stick may attract moisture and a non porous stirrer which can be thrown away afterwards would be better.

When the ratio of resin to catalyst has been calculated the two are mixed together which starts the irreversable chemical reaction that turns the liquid to a solid. Where the catalyst is measured out by drops it is added directly to the resin. In order to avoid *uncatalysed* resin being poured into a mould, always add the catalyst before colouring or embedding objects in the resin. This may not be the case where thickners or other additives are used in which case the catalyst is added last (see overleaf).

Stir gently and thoroughly.

The *pot-life* or working time of catalysed resin is around 15 to 20 minutes so there is not a great rush. The resin goes through stages as it is curing; from a liquid to a jelly like substance, at this stage it can no longer be used or poured. The time taken for it to turn to jelly is known as the *'gel time.'* This is affected by the ambient temperature, the higher it is the faster the resin sets. The best temperature is between 18°C and 21°C (44°F and 70°F). It may not set properly below the minimum temperature.

Once you have mixed your resin it is then ready to take additives.

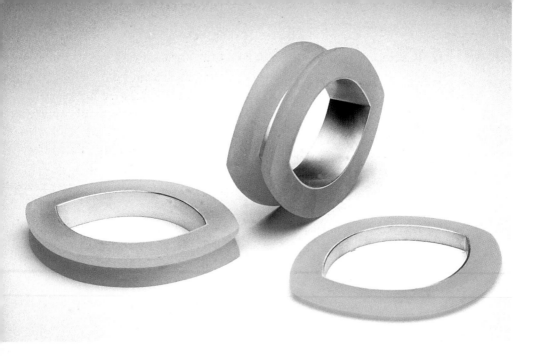

**Sarah King (England)**
Bangles, resin and silver, 1999.
Photo Graham Murrell.

it may require a more flexible mould material. Where no filing or other finishing technique is to be applied to the surface of the casting this will dictate the type of resin used in the mould as well as the mould material. Most plastics will reproduce the surface finish of the mould into which they have been cast. Polyester resin tends to become glossy on the surface after it has been removed from the mould, where the mould material has inhibited the full cure of the resin. Polyester resins with a high wax content come out looking quite matt rather than glossy as the wax helps it to cure. Polyurethane and epoxy resin will reproduce the surface finish in most cases but results will vary depending on the type used.

Other factors affecting the choice of mould material will be the number of times a casting needs to be reproduced and where a resin has a high exotherm it may be necessary to cool the mould and draw the heat away.

## Flexible materials

**Silicone rubber** A fairly expensive and non-reusable mould material but readily available in small quantities. An easy to use and less hazardous mould making material. A cold cure rubber with excellent detailing and which requires no release agent. Like polyester resin it is a liquid which is cured by means of a catalyst but does not produce an exotherm and comes in a number of forms from very runny to thixotropic. Its curing time can vary from 20 minutes to 30 hours, fully curing after a few days. Follow the manufacturer's directions for correct mixing proportions. It will adhere to itself, so can be poured in layers if necessary, conversely, a spray release agent is also available and can be used to prevent layers sticking to one another. Many castings can be taken from the one mould, the first few resin pieces taken from the mould may have a tacky surface but this could be due to rubber still releasing some vapours. It can withstand temperatures from -50° to +250°C (-58°F to +482°F) making it ideal for the high exotherms produced while resin is curing. The silicone rubber can be placed in a vacuum machine to remove all the air bubbles from it.

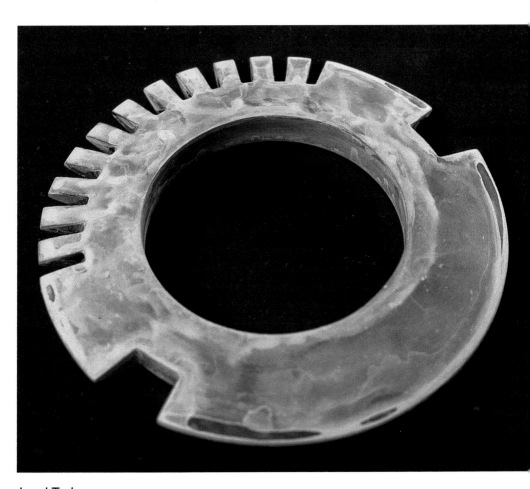

**Jared Taylor**
Bangle, resin, 1992.
Photo K.S. Murphy.

source. On top of this is placed a heatproof dish that has been smeared with detergent, to act as a release, containing an evenly spread layer of polyethylene granules. Once the granules have melted, this takes about 30 minutes and the granules become one clear mass, leave the whole thing to cool. The sheet can then be cut up into individual pieces of the right size when needed. The master needs to be made of silver or an aluminium alloy, the shape being very simple with a limited number of undercuts and quite shallow, not more than 2cm deep. The master is then warmed on a steel plate. Again, a smear of detergent over the master will act as a release. When the master is warmed through, the polyethylene sheet is placed over the master and will take on the master shape as the heat softens it. Chase out any air and then cool the master and mould under a fan.

**Wood and Plaster** can both be used as a mould material but being porous need to be prepared with release agents to prevent the resin sticking. They also need to be sealed first, especially if there may be some moisture, using primer sealer such as G4. A coating of wax release is then put on top of this. The mould shape can be male or female depending on which surface needs to be smooth. More suited to large constructions rather than jewellery, but there may be some form that it is suited to. See the example in chapter five under Thixotropic.

# Materials used in making masters

Here too there are a number of materials that can be used in making masters. Certain materials are more obtainable than others. What your master is made of is not necessarily of paramount importance. Where a perfect result is required the master must be made in a material that can be polished and used in conjunction with a mould material such as silicone rubber that picks up very good surface detailing. The better the master the less cleaning up on the cast resin piece afterwards. The master needs to be slightly larger than the required size of the final piece, as firstly the resin shrinks around 10 to 20% and then filing and finishing will remove more material. In most cases the master can be used repeatedly to make several moulds of the same shape. Some materials will be more long-lasting than others.

The shape of your master will determine what mould material you can use. A master shape with deep undercuts and recess will require a flexible mould material. It is worth including any recesses which are part of the design in the master so that a hole need not be drilled later on. This avoids having to remove material or drill/burr an awkward area.

**Wood** Masters are quick to make

Examples of masters in MDF and milliput that have been sprayed with primer with the resin castings from the masters beside them. Photo William Teakle.

# Closed moulds

A little thought has to be given when making a closed mould. (See the example on the following pages.)

The shape of the master may prevent a closed mould being made from it. Once the shape is enclosed in the rubber it has to be cut out of there with a minimum number of cuts.

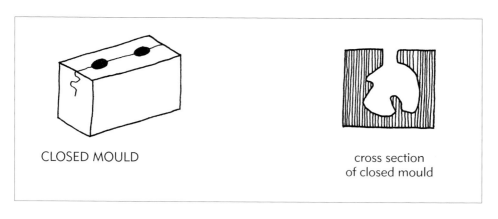

CLOSED MOULD

cross section
of closed mould

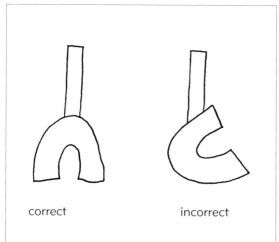

correct                    incorrect

Sprueing the master.

Where the rubber closes back on itself it will leave a join line if there has been an uneven cutting line. *The pouring hole* must not be lower than any part of the master. As the liquid resin is poured in through the hole, it will settle out under gravity and any air bubbles in the resin will rise to the highest point. A pouring hole is created by adding a sprue to the master using dowling or a rod. It may be necessary to add a second sprue in the mould, this hole will act as a vent allowing air to escape. A master set at the wrong angle on the sprue may result in the mould producing incomplete castings where the air cannot escape easily or the liquid settles out at too low a level.

# Skin moulds

A combination of the above two mould types, either made of latex or thixotropic silicone rubber, useful where a master with a lot of detailing may require a flexible mould that can easily be peeled off, or you need to economise on how much silicone rubber is used. The mould may need some kind of support when filled with liquid resin. To make sure that the shape does not distort, the outside of the skin mould can be set in plaster.

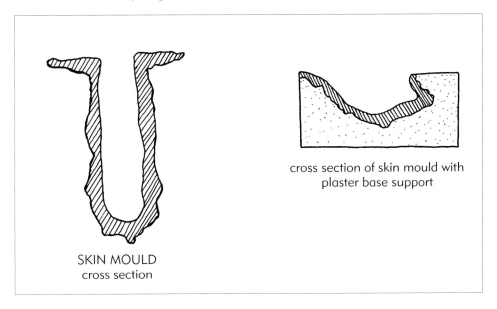

SKIN MOULD
cross section

cross section of skin mould with
plaster base support

If required, vacuum the rubber now to remove all air bubbles and then pour into the mould. Tap gently to release any air if not already vacuumed. Leave to set for 24 hours.

Once set remove the base. You should know from your note which way your piece is sitting inside the rubber. Try and make your cutting line around the centre of the piece to allow for easy removal. Using a sharp scalpel make a shallow incision, hold the rubber apart under tension and continue irregular shallow cuts and along the edge, use a wedge shaped cut into the rubber to act as a locating point. Do not cut all the way down the mould sides but to a point around half way where the master can be removed easily.

## SKIN MOULDS

These illustrate the use of alginate, plaster and thixotropic silicone paste.

Cover the part of the body in the alginate. This sets very quickly.

Mix up the plaster and fill the alginate mould. Work between fingers to release air. Leave to set.

Seal the plaster master with primer and then apply several wax coatings. Fix to a base. Mix up the thixotropic silicone rubber and then paste up over the master. It may need another layer.

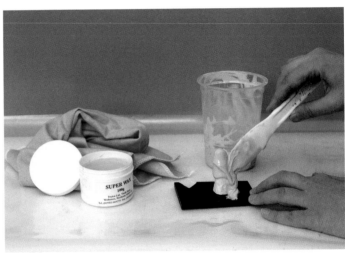

Find something to support the skin mould, brass tubing has been used in the photograph, or cut a hole in a piece of cardboard and use it to support the collar of the mould. It is ready to fill with resin.

All photos by William Teakle.

Having removed some of the resin from the casting surface, small areas where bubbles have broken the surface may become apparent. At this stage it is possible to fill these in using a small quantity of resin dropped in using a wire or pin. Do not worry that the resin is now cloudy and white looking on the surface, as it is worked and the resin becomes smoother the colour returns.

A faster method of removing material would be to use a linicher. Remember these machines can cut away very quickly and plastic is a relatively soft material, dust extraction and a mask are essential.

## Papering

If the surface of the resin is not very tacky and full of bubbles it is possible to move straight to this stage. Starting with the coarsest of wet and dry papers, p320 and working your way through the grades (grits) to the finest at p1200. Use the paper with water, i.e. wet, this keeps the dust down and removes the debris easily. Remember to rinse the piece off between each grade, any stray piece of coarse grit will mark the surface.

P1200 will produce a very fine surface which is slightly matt, it can be left as finished at this stage. Matt finishes on resin can be acheived by using pumice powder in a stone barreller or by sand blasting, if you have access to a machine.

The colour of the resin can be brought out in a matt piece by rubbing a moisturiser or body oil into the surface. Any matt piece of resin will pick up body oils and become shiny over time, although it is not as harsh as a polished shine.

## Polishing

A finely papered surface will polish up very easily. This can be done by hand or by machine. By hand, although more laborious, a bright shine can be acheived using a liquid metal polish such as Brasso or Autosol.

A polishing machine will also remove material as well as polish. A cutting compound for plastics is available, which will remove some material but not a great deal. A hard polished finish can be obtained with cotton mops and wool mops using Vonax or stainless steel polishing compound or other products available from resin suppliers. Use different mops for different compounds and clean the object being polished in between compounds.

The photograph shows the angle at which to hold your work when polishing on a machine. Keep the piece moving constantly to prevent the resin surface being cut into and also to prevent burning from frictional heat at the point of contact. This results in the surface becoming cloudy and roughening. The area will then have to be

Polishing, hold the piece to the mop at the level shown, remembering to keep the piece moving. Photo William Teakle.

repapered, as the machine does not polish it out. Plastic is not as hard as metal and polishing requires less pressure on the object against the mop.

## Lathing resin

For some reason it may be necessary to lathe a piece of resin rather than cast it in the shape already required by lathing the shape in another material to form a master. To lathe resin the plastic is normally turned dry but oil can be used as a lubricant. The tools should be sharpened as for soft metals and angled as for cutting aluminium. The tool should not chip the work as it cuts. The turning speed should be slow, at around 300rpm.

**Cicada**

Bangle, necklace and earrings.

These pieces were made by burring the pattern into acrylic or resin and then filling it with another coloured resin. Photo courtesy Brighton University.

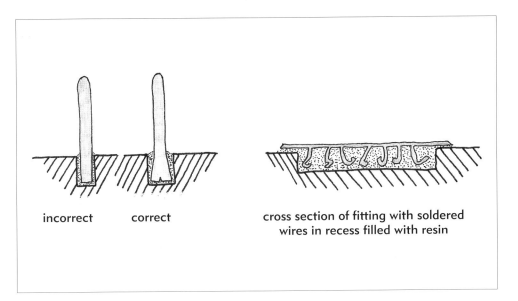

**incorrect**     **correct**

**cross section of fitting with soldered
wires in recess filled with resin**

Metal fittings set in resin.

ways of attatching other materials to resin other than by glue or adhesive. The surfaces of all materials must be keyed and free of oils and grease. Resin will adhere very well to itself and can be used to trap metal fittings in a hole or recess which is then filled with resin (see above). The metal will need to be deeply scored, pinned, or a flange made in the metal to prevent it from coming out of the resin. Resin does not stick to metal and will not form a strong bond where a simple contact join is made. For fittings that are to be stuck on to the surface of the piece it is imperative that the two surfaces are well scored to prevent them shearing away.

Other adhesives that can be used are epoxy or polyurethane ones which form very strong bonds. If necessary they can be coloured, a miniscule amount of colour paste can be added, but not too much as it will affect the bond strength. Use it sparingly – great globs of glue are unsightly. Superglue or cyanoacrylate will stick metal to resin on a small scale, such as an earring post, but it can form a brittle bond and is very nasty stuff on human skin and the fumes can affect the eyes.

**Kathie Murphy**
Earrings, resin and rubber, 1995.
Photo K.S. Murphy

# CHAPTER SIX

# Using resin

## Colour

Colour is added to resin by using pigment pastes particularly made for colouring resin. They come in a concentrated form and disperse easily in resin. Available in either opaque or transparent form and a wide variety of colours. They can be intermixed to create hues and other colours. It is advisable to use these pigments as other methods of colouring, such as using oil paints, may lead to the resin not curing properly. The pastes are lightfast and designed not to alter colour with the heat of the plastic polymerising. It is possible to buy them in as small a

**Carla Edwards**
Bangles, resin, 1999.
Photo C. Edwards.

Example of the gradation of colour in resin from one paste colour that has been added in slightly increased quantities. Note the very small amount on the end of the mixing stick. Photo William Teakle.

uncatalysed pre-activated resin and store it in a suitable container. Add the catalyst to the coloured resin as and when you need it.

To create a pattern of colour within the resin it should be done using one batch of catalysed resin. Avoid mixing resins that are undergoing the exothermic reaction at differing rates. Mix the quantity required, say 100 ml of resin and then divide this into four seperate pots, or the number of different colours required. Each pot has a sperate colour mixed in it. Then pour each colour into the mould, an open mould would be best as then it is possible to see and control where each colour is going. A wire can be

used to pull the colours into each other. Some colour bleeding may occur, it may be necessary to use a resin that is more viscous to prevent the colours homogenising.

Pattern can also be created by pouring one colour into another and using gravity and the movement of the liquids to create a simple juxtaposition of colours.

Fluorescent colours are available that have been designed for use in industrial plastics. The correct type of powder is required to ensure that it mixes with polyester resin. To prevent lumps of powder forming in the resin transfer a small quantity of a resin mix into another pot and stir thoroughly, once there are no lumps

**Robert Johnstone**
Vase, resin, 1998.
Photo Cheryl Twomey.

**Sarah Stafford**
Bangle, silver and resin, 2000.
Photo Norman Hollands.

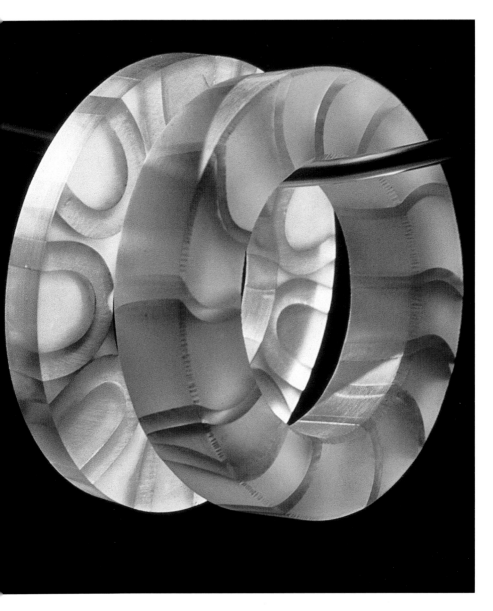

**Carla Edwards**
Bangles, resin, paper and acrylic, 1998.
Photo John K. McGregor.

upside down in the resin, if the bottom of the mould will end up being the top of the casting. To prevent the object from rising to the surface, which it is likely to do as resin is a liquid, it is advisable to cast in layers. To avoid air bubbles being trapped in the cast pour the resin in carefully and tease out any air with a thin piece of wire. With a porous object, any air will be chased out by pouring in layers. Pour the next layer on a piece when the surface is still tacky. More detailed considerations are given below under the type of item to be embedded.

**Flora and fauna** It has long been popular to encapsulate and preserve flowers or insects in resin but in order for the result to be successful the item must be completley dry and free of moisture and oils. Resin does not like moisture, it is possible to set for example a fresh tomato in resin but over time it will shrink away from the resin and deteriorate, the moisture in it may cause the resin to go cloudy too. Another factor is that the heat generated by the curing resin may affect the colour in the flower or insect.

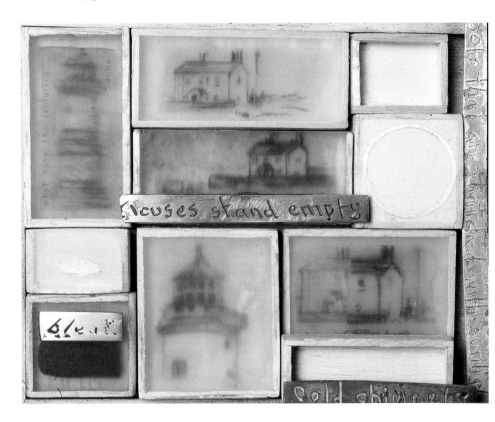

**Elizabeth J. Abbey**
*The Lighthouse Brooch*, resin, drawing on paper, wood and metal, 1999.
Photo Don Williams.

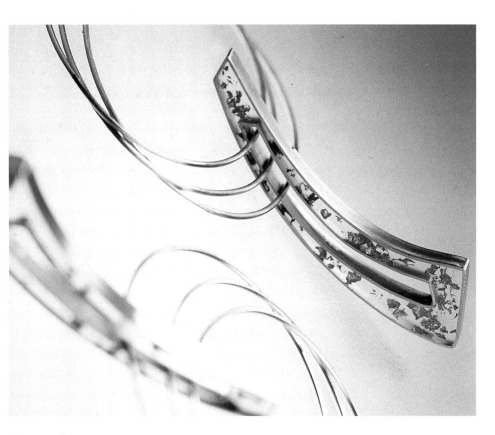

**Miranda Sharpe**
Bangles, silver, resin and gold leaf.
Photo Stephen Lenthall.

To preserve flowers the simplest method is to press them and avoid any damp conditions. The colour should remain but will not be light fast. It may be possible to add colour afterwards or coat the surface in a polyurethane varnish to protect the flower and bring out the colour. Other methods of preserving flora are by slowly drying out the specimen in an oven on a low heat, or by placing them in a tightly sealed container with silica gel and leaving it undisturbed in a warm dry area until all the moisture is absorbed by the silica. In researching this book I came across a recipe for dehydrating natural specimens, it has not been tested. The specimens are immersed in a series of solutions, starting with a solution of 50% alcohol to water, followed by 70%, 90% and finally pure alcohol. Each phase requires that the specimen is left for a period of 10 to 12 hours until all the moisture has been replaced. Freeze dried flowers can be bought by mail order, saving time and disappointment.

Any insect that is to be set in resin must have the natural oils removed by degreasing using acetone. Do not

**Robert Johnstone**
Pendants, resin, paper and foil, 1995.
Photo Stephen Byrne.

ruin your favourite specimen, carry out some tests first on others.

**Paper** Some types may need to be sealed with a laquer to prevent the dyes in the paper from bleeding.

**Foils** Can be used in resin to great effect. It can be awkward controlling the very thin foils, particularly if the resin has a static charge on it. Some metals are also not ideal for use in resin, ferrous metals tend to oxidise and need to be sealed, silver reacts with resin oxidising the silver and in

some instances discolouring the resin. Gold has no reaction to resin.

**Stones** These can be set in resin to create a material such as terrazzo. As long as the stone is fairly soft, it can be worked without the softer plastic area being worn down faster than the material that has been embedded.

**Plastics** As mentioned in the mould making section, some plastics will not adhere to resin and would not be suitable for use in resin embedding. Polystyrene is also unsuitable as it dissolves in contact with resin. The heat from the

**Mary Farrell**
Earrings, resin and foil, 1997.

81

**Ted Noten**
Necklace, acrylic, resin and rings.
Photo Ted Noten.

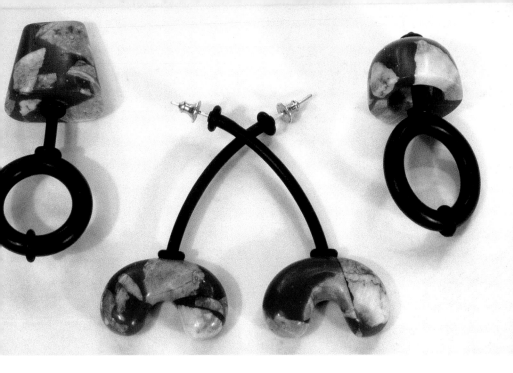

**Kathie Murphy**
Rings and earrings, resin and marble(terrazzo) with rubber, 1990.
Photo K. S. Murphy.

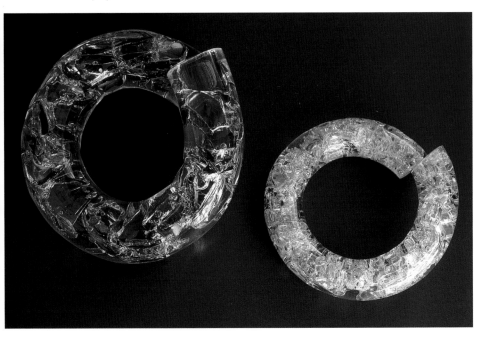

**Pamina (England)**
Bangles, resin, bottle glass and windscreen glass, 2000.
Photo K. S. Murphy.

83

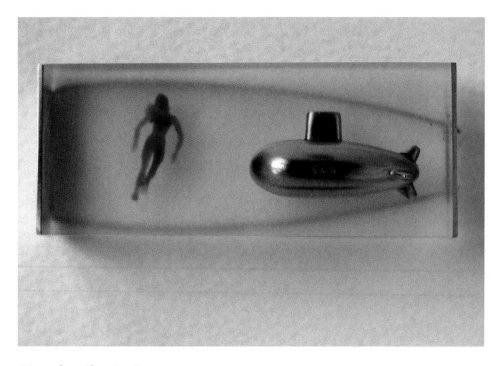

**Eileen Gatt (Scotland)**
Brooch, resin, metal and plastic, 1997.
Photo E. Gatt.

**Dawn Gulyas (England)**
Brooch, resin and gold, 1998.
Photo Joël Degen.

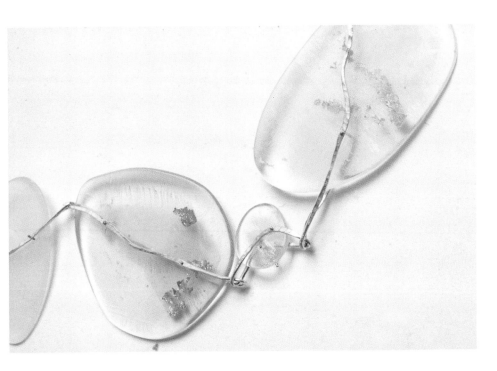

**Nelly Kallirosi (Greece)**
Necklace detail, resin, fabric and foil, 1998.
Photo P. Kallirosi.

**Sarah Stafford**
Silver and resin, 2000.
Photo Norman Hollands.

exothermic reaction may cause crazing in acrylics, but this could be used for effect. Carry out some tests on different plastics if you are not sure of its type. Remember to take into account the shrinkage of the resin so that it does not pull away from the embedded material's surface.

**Fabric and other such materials can be used too.**

Instead of embedding an object it is also possible to create air pockets within the resin. Certain plastics will not stick to resin and it is possible to use these to create a cavity by embedding them in the resin and then removing them afterwards. A bit of thought will have to be given as to how to extract them from the set resin. It is also possible to use clay to form a space, the clay can then be removed from the cast resin by scraping it out.

# Fillers

There are different reasons for using fillers in resin. It may be to cut down the cost by using less resin which is bulked out by the filler, to imitate another material like metal or marble, or to enhance the colour after pigmentation. All come in the form of powders and must be dry. If you are not sure of how the powder will affect the resin then carry out a small test first.

**Kate Groombridge**
Locket, resin, 1999.
Photo K. Groombridge.

When calculating the amount of catalyst required for a filled resin it is done on the resin content alone.

Calcium carbonate is used where a reduced amount of resin is needed. It has a whitening effect on any pigments that are added and can also improve the resistance and wear of the resin. Roughly equal parts by volume of resin and filler are used.

**Slate and marble powder** are used to simulate the natural materials.

**Sintered metals** can be added to resin to create the effect of real metal. They are fine particles of metal and not a pigment. It can add quite a weight to your piece depending on the size of your casting. To avoid anything too heavy the sintered metals can be used as a gel coat layer. The surface of the resin/metal cast can be patinated afterwards. When calculating the resin to metal powder mix: by **volume** it is done by nearly equal parts with slightly more metal and by **weight** an approximate guide is shown below:

*Resin: Copper-4/1*
*Resin: Aluminium-1.25/1*
*Resin: Bronze-6/1*

for other metal (brass and iron) proportions ask the supplier.

Use any mix of resin and metal powder immediately, do not store it for future use. Some resins may be better suited to a metal filler than

**Metal Powder Filler** Here the weight ratio of metal powder to resin was calculated, also shown is a casting made using sintered bronze powder. Photo William Teakle.

another. For all metals, other than aluminium, catalyst is added at 2%, for aluminium it is added at 1%.

**Avoid inhaling the powders. Aluminium powder is explosive and all safety data should be read before use.**

# Thixotropic

A resin with a low viscosity can be used as a surface or gelcoat, it would not be suitable for pouring into a cast. Very light and bulky pieces can be created using a core of polyurethane foam or balsa wood with layers of resin built up over the surface.

The resin can be coloured in the usual way and finished as with cast pieces.

Jesmonite can be made thixotropic. The thickener is added slowly, drop by drop to the mixture as it is very reactive, until the desired consistency has been reached.

Another method of using thixotropic resin would be over a plaster, wood or solid rubber master to create a hollow piece in reinforced resin. The master in wood or plaster would have to be waxed to prevent the resin sticking and be simple with no undercuts to aid removal from inside the reinforced resin outer shell.

One layer of glassfibre tissue or roving and resin is layed up over the master and allowed to set. By carefully cutting around the set GRP (glass reinforced plastic) the master can then be removed from

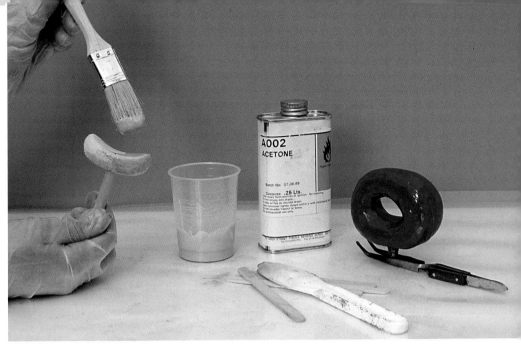

**Thixotropic Resin** A Gel coat resin is brushed on to a balsa wood master, the acetone is used for cleaning the brush only. The large blue oval object is balsa with four coats of resin. Photo William Teakle.

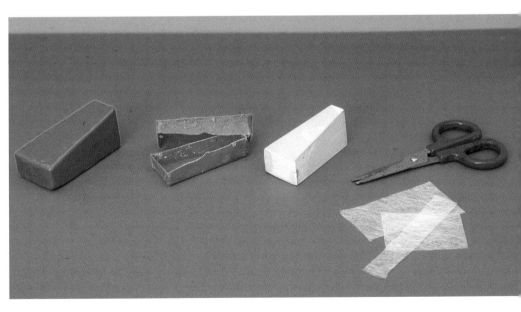

**Thixotropic Resin and Glass Fibre** Shown is glass fibre tissue and the wood and Milliput master (waxed) with the first layer of resin and fibre that has been cut away from the master. The left-hand orange object is the final hollow piece, three more layers of fibre and resin were added.
Photo William Teakle.

**Dawn Gulyas**
Neckpiece, resin, whitemetal and steel, 1997.
Photo Joel Degen.

inside. The now hollow resin halves can be reassembled and joined by adding more glassfibre and resin, slowly building up another few layers to create a strong hollow piece. Do not wait for each layer to completely cure before adding the next layer, but sand down inbetween to ensure an even surface. **Handle the fibreglass with care, wear protective clothing and a mask.**

# Electroforming

This is the process whereby a deposit of metal is built up in layers on the surface of a finished piece, made in metal or *another* material. By passing an electric current through an electrolytic solution of metal salts anode. This causes the metal ions in solution to become positvely charged and travel toward a negatively charged cathode, which is the object to be plated. A substantial layer of metal can be built up, enough to make the resulting electroform, when not plated onto metal, feel solid.

**Diana Greenwood (England)**
Brooches, silverplated resin, 1998.
Photo D. Greenwood.

**James Cox (England)**
Hat, electroformed resin with zinc
passivated finish, 1986. Photo J. Cox

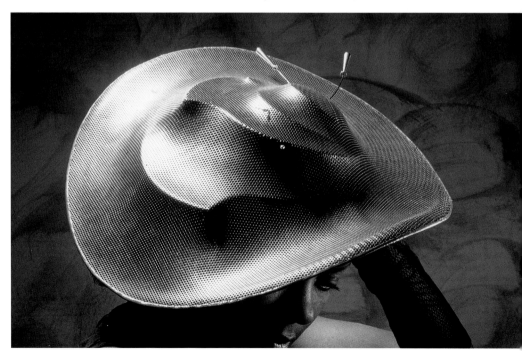

91

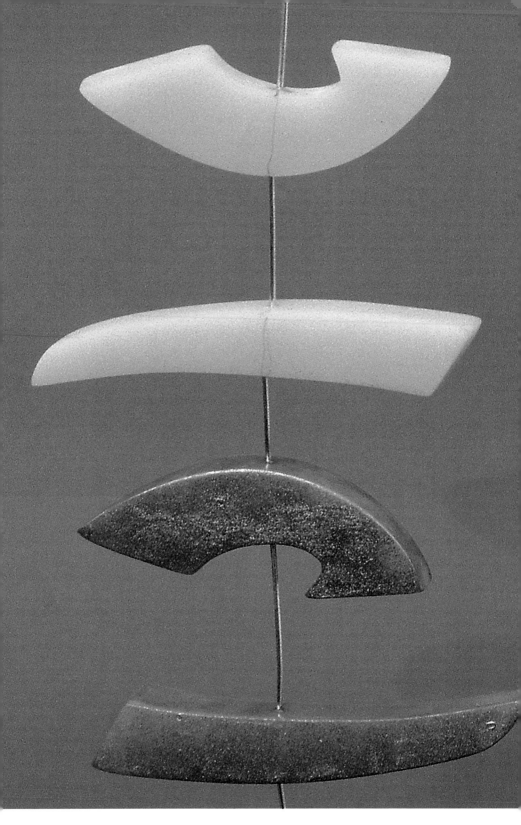

Resin can be used as a model over which to electroform, creating a metal object with a resin core. As it is a light material it can be used to create large designs not suitable to be fully constructed out of metal, as they would be too heavy. The resin model is quite quick to prepare and a high finish is possible, the metal coating picks up any surface detail on the model. Plastics are non-conductive and therefore need to be coated in a metallic laquer (electrodag) in order to make the surface conductive. An electroplating company can usually do this for you. It is possible to do the plating yourself should you have the facilities but as silver plating involves the use of cyanide, it may be preferable to leave it to someone else. Once the piece has been plated and removed from the bath (electrolytic solution) the metal can look quite matt if special brightners have not been added to the solution, this can be overcome by gently burnishing the metal plate with a wire brush and detergent.

Points to consider when designing resin pieces to be electroformed;

The resin core will not allow soldering once the piece has been plated.

Resin pieces being prepared for the plating bath, the bottom two have a copper laquer painted on the surface of the resin. The silver wire acts as a conductor between the pieces. Photo William Teakle.

The shape of the piece to be plated will influence where the deposit of metal will build up. Flat surfaces tend to get a greater build up around the edges, particularly if they are squared. A rounded edge is more likely to produce an even plating. Convex shapes are plated more evenly than concave. Protrusions or peaks will build up a thicker layer.

The whole surface of the resin need not be plated, a metal deposit will only build up where the metallic laquer has been sprayed or painted. This could be used to good effect in a design.

# Cold enamelling

A less expensive way of enamelling is to use resin, called cold enamelling as a kiln is not needed. The best type of resin would be one with a low exotherm and shrinkage, epoxy resins are best in this respect. If that is not available then a resin which dries as tack free as possible. Smaller quantities are mixed with this technique so check that the resin is suitable for use in small volume. Generally with epoxy it is used in a 2:1 ratio. It is possible to use a polyester resin although its shrinkage rate means that it could come away from surrounding surfaces. To avoid this happening, use up to 2% catalyst but no more. Follow the usual procedure and add the desired colour paste. It is possible to use the resin for the different types of enamelling.

**Cold Enamelling** *Plique à jour* resin is placed in the tubing and allowed to set. The Plasticine base stops the resin from leaking out.
Photo William Teakle.

*Plique-à-jour* can be acheived more easily using resin than glass enamel. The piece of work has no backing to it which means that light can pass through. When preparing the area to be filled with resin it will be necessary to provide a temporary backing to contain the resin while it sets. A material such as Plasticine can be used, it is mouldable and the resin does not adhere to it. Alternatively masking tape may be enough where the casting is very shallow. Once an area has been filled and allowed to set, any discrepancy in height can be increased by adding a little more resin. The resin once cured can be finished using wet and dry papers and then polished.

*Cloisonné or champlevé* can also be easily acheived using resin. The recesses should be clean and a key given to the surface of the metal, this can be used to effect by texturing the metal using a burr or milling, which will then show through any transparent resin. To avoid air bubbles getting trapped it is suggested that a small amount of resin is brushed into any corners or recesses before pouring in the rest and a meniscus is created in the resin to prevent the under filling of the cavity. When using resin as an enamel in silver the surface may need to be treated in order to prevent the resin from discolouring the silver. The photograph of Zoe Frantzeskou's brooches shows one where the resin and silver has discoloured while the resin set at the same time into the gold plated cavity has remained clear and the gold unaffected.

**Betty Heald (USA)**
Brooches, silver and
epoxy resin, 2001.
Photo Norman Watkins.

94

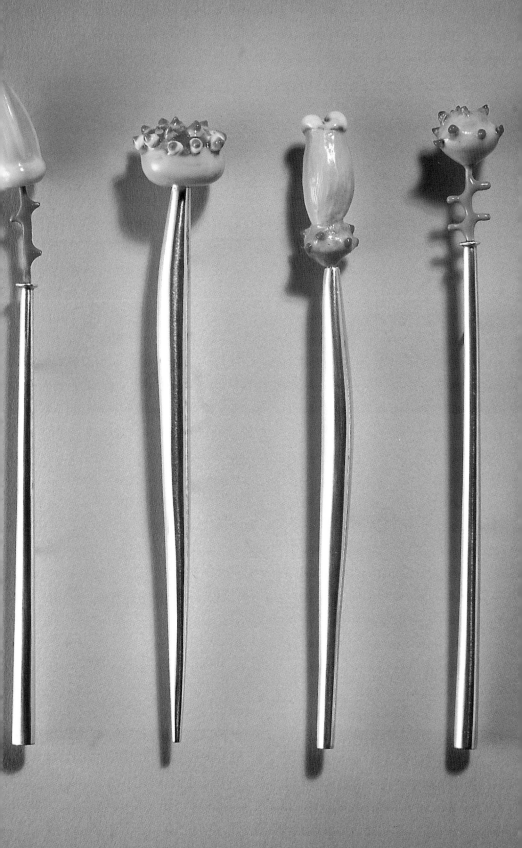

**Zoe Frantzeskou**
The top left-hand brooch is silver that has been filled with clear resin, over time the silver and the resin have discoloured. The bottom righthand brooch is goldplated silver and here the gold has not been affected and neither has the resin, 1998. Photo P. Papavasilou.

**Cicada (England)**
Necklace and earrings, resin and acrylic tubing, 1980. Photo P. Thornton.

**(ABOVE) Juliet Sheath (England)**
Necklace, rings, cufflinks and earrings, resin and silver, 1998.
Photo Robert Hall.

**Diana King (England)**
Brooch/hat pins, resin and silver, 1999.
Photo Scott Talbott.

**Cold Enamelling Cloisonnè**, different
coloured resins are poured into the
seperate sections of a piece made up
in frosted acrylic.
Photo William Teakle.

**Sarah King**
Rings, resin and silver, 1999.
Photo Graham Murrell.

# CHAPTER SEVEN

# Small objects and further applications in resin

It is a short step from jewellery to small objects made in resin such as small objects for the home, doorhandles, lights, trays, containers and cutlery.

**Louise Hibbert (Wales)**
*Cephalopholis Box I*, sycamore, walnut veneer, acrylic ink and polyester resin, 1999. Photo Tony Boase.

**Louise Hibbert**
*Radiolarian Vessel III* (detail), 1998.
Photo Frank Youngs.

**Cara Croninger**
Dish resin 1995.
Photo Bruce Schwarz.

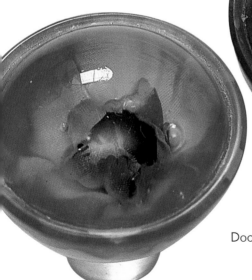

**Corinna Julnes (England)**
Door handles, resin and fabric flowers, 1998.
Photo Kathie Murphy.

**Helen Stuart (England)**
Vessels, resin and metals, 1999.
Photo H. Stuart.

103

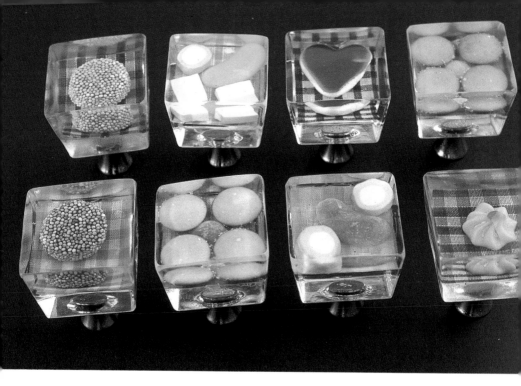

**Corinna Julnes (England)**
Drawer handles, resin and sweets, 1998.
Photo Kathie Murphy.

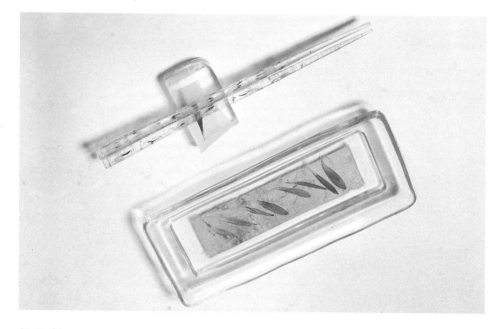

**Katie New**
Sushi dish, resin, foil and leaves, 1999.
Photo David Burton.

**Tom Kirk (England)**
*Lightbox*, steel and resin, 1999.
Photo Tom Kirk.

**James Cox**
Electroformed door furniture for The Crafts Council, 1993.
Photo J. Cox.


**Robert Johnstone**
Vase, resin, silver and gold leaf, 1998.
Photo Cheryl Twomey

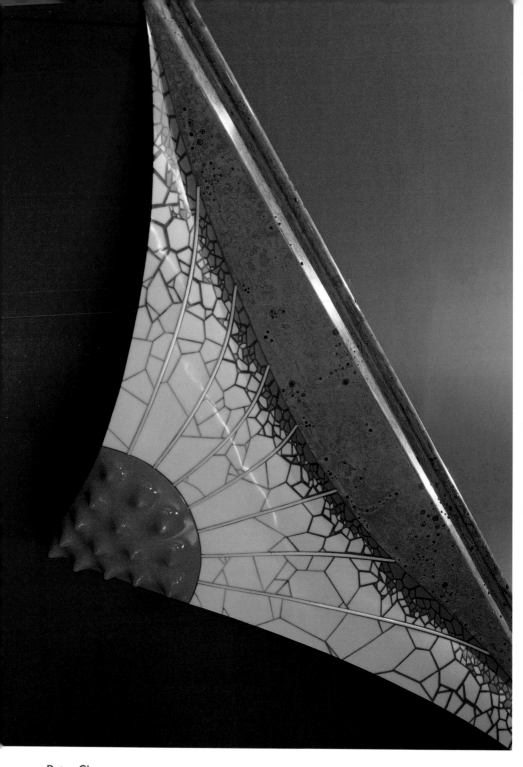

**Peter Chang**
Handrail for Inverness Gallery, art-tm, polyester and acrylic, 1997/98.
Photo P. Chang.

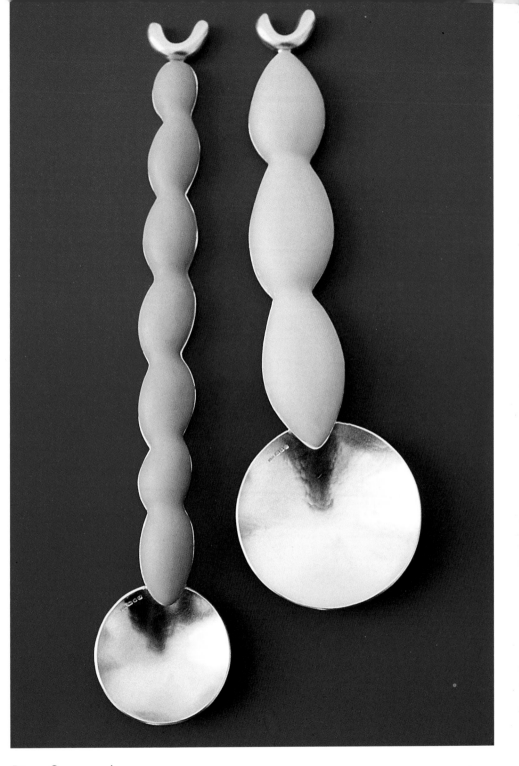

**Diana Greenwood**
Spoons, silver and resin, 1999.
Photo D. Greenwood.

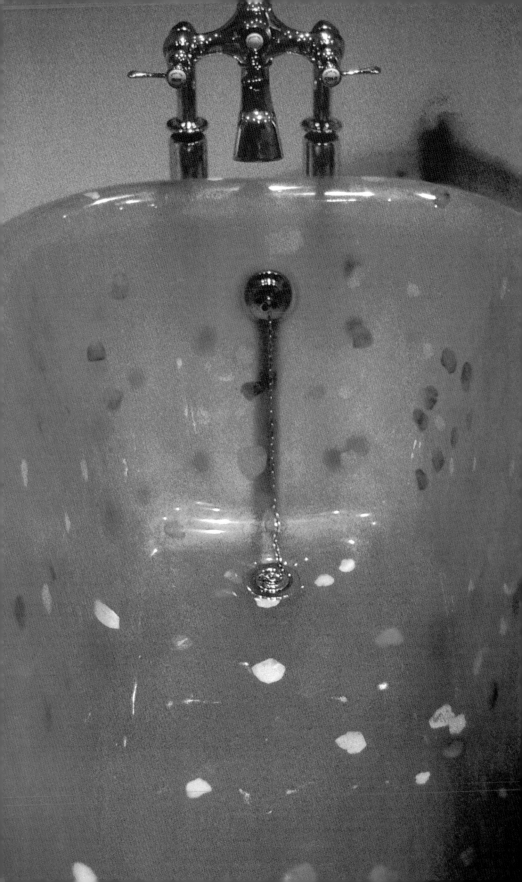

**Naomi Rae (England)**
Bathtub, GRP and roses.

Peter Chang has recently completed a handrail in resin and other plastics for the Inverness Gallery, art.tm, and James Cox made the handles at the Crafts Council from electroformed resin.

Diana Greenwood who made the electroformed silver brooches went on to make the cutlery pictured (see page 109) using opaque resin for the handles. Robert Johnstone's intricately inlaid and textured jewellery led to him creating larger surface areas of the resin and making them into containers.

Larger applications in resin are exemplified by Naomi Rae's design, which changed the mundane and homogenously coloured GRP bathtub into something quite different by setting rosepetals in a lightly tinted transparent glass-

**Naomi Rae**
Bathtub (detail).
Photo Jaqui Caley.

**Jo Mills (England)**
*Fountain piece I,* rapid prototype epoxy resin, 1999.
Photo Jo Mills.

reinforced resin. Computer technology has created the bowl by Jo Mills. A computer aided design is transfered into a stereolithography file which can be read by the computer of a rapid prototyping machine. The machine contains a bath of liquid epoxy resin. The piece is created by the computer making a laser beam flash through the resin, where the flash occurs it sets solid. It is a slow process, the bowl pictured took eight hours, as the object is built up in thousands of layers. The piece is then cured in an oven for 40 minutes. The solid epoxy becomes unstable and distorts after a short time, to make the object last it is possible to electroform over it. Rapid prototyping is more usually used in the car industry for trying out new designs but used here, intricate and very fine designs can be created in the material that cannot be achieved by other methods.

**Emma Langley**
*Triplicate,* polyester resin and fibreglass, 2001.
Photo Emma Langey.

**Emma Langley**
*Succelents,* resin, fibreglass and flocking, 2001.
Photo Emma Langey.

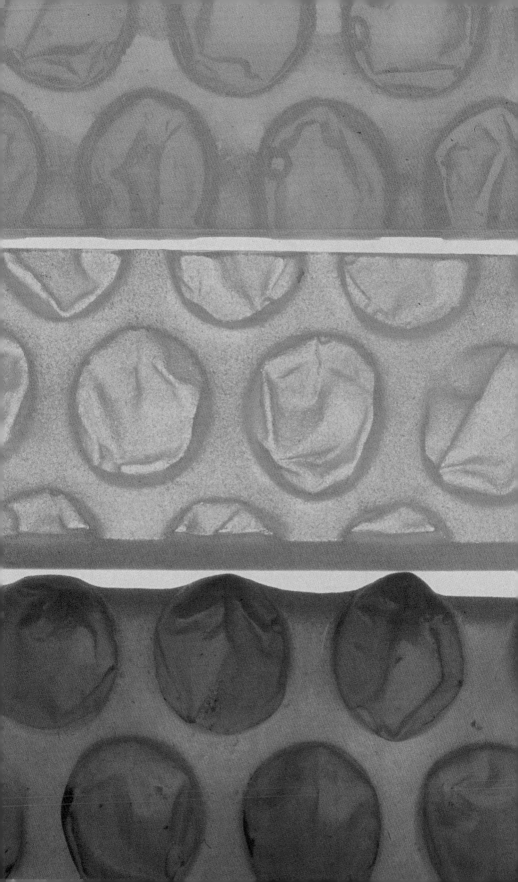

# Glossary

**Accelerator**
A mixture that speeds up the chemical reaction or polymerisation of the resin.

**Acetone**
Chemical solvent used to clean off uncured resin from brushes and other implements. *Highly flammable*, it should be stored safely and used in a well ventilated area.

**Activator**
*See* accelerator.

**Barrier cream**
Product used for protecting skin.

**Cabosil**
A trade name for a type of silica sand. It is used as a thickening or thixotropic agent in resins.

**Catalyst**
Added to resin in small quantities to initiate polymerisation or exothermic reaction.

**Carla Edwards**
Brooch (detail), resin, 1998
Photo John K. McGregor.

**Cold Enamelling**
Term used where resin is used as a coating in place of glass enamel which has to be kiln fired.

**Curing**
Process by which plastic or resin hardens.

**Embed**
To fix something firmly in a surrounding mass.

**Exothermic reaction**
A chemical reaction that gives off heat. Most resins generate heat as they react with the catalyst during the curing process.

**Flash point**
The temperature at which something will catch fire, used to define its flammability. Liquid resin has a flash point of 21-55°C and is classified as flammable.

**Gel**
Stage at which resin turns from liquid to solid and forms jelly-like substance.

## Gel coat
A thixotropic resin and also the term used for thin resin coating applied to the surface as a decorative finish.

## Hardener
or curing agent, a substance added to epoxy or polyurethane resins in specific quantities to change them from a liquid to a solid.

## MEKP
Abbreviation of Methyl Ethyl Ketone Peroxide. An organic oxidising agent and the most commonly used catalyst for curing polyester resins. *Handle with care.*

## Methyl methacrylate
Otherwise known as acrylic.

## Oxidising agent
A substance which effects oxidation by adding oxygen or removing hydrogen when chemically reacting with certain materials.

## Pearlescence
Having a pearl like appearance.

## Polymerisation
The process by which monomers join up to form long chains to form a polymer. Synthetic plastics are derived from polymers.

## Pot life
The working time possible from the point at which the catalyst or hardener is added to the resin to the point at which the resin is no longer

pourable and begins to gel.

## Release agent
A chemical or mixture that is used on a surface or added to the uncured resin to prevent the adhesion of the resin to the mould.

## RTV
Usually found on silicone rubber products it stands for room-temperature vulcanising.

## Sprue
The piece of dowling or rod that is used to create a pouring hole for the liquid resin in the mould. In some instances it may be necessary to add another sprue so that the air can escape from the mould, acting as a vent.

## Thermosetting plastic
A plastic that undergoes an irreversible chemical reaction to set solid. They cannot be reheated to return to their original state like a thermoplastics.

## Thixotropic
A term used to describe a non-runny substance. Resin that is thixotropic will remain in place on an upright surface until it has cured. Additives, such as Cabosil and special resins can be used in a liquid resin to make it thixotropic.

## Translucent
A term which means that some light might pass through but that it is not

transparent or see-through.

## Vacuum chamber
A machine which removes unwanted air trapped in a mixture. Most often used to remove bubbles from silicone rubber that is to be used to make a very accurate mould.

## Vacuum forming
The method by which a clamped sheet of thermo plastic is heated until soft and then pulled down over a master or perforated form, at this stage a vacuum sucks the softened sheet around the master or form. The master or form is removed and the plastic sheet can be used as a mould for resin. Only plastics such as PVC or polythene can be used as they do not react with resin.

## Viscosity
The fluidity of a liquid. Low viscosity means that it will pour or flow readily. High viscosity means that it will be sticky, thixotropic and not pourable.

# Useful Addresses-Resin and Rubbers

Most Companies have good technical support departments, technical data, and supply health and safety information.

## UK

Ambersil Ltd
Jacobsen House
The Crossways
Castlefield Industrial Estate
Bridgewater
Somerset
TA6 4DD
Tel: 01278 424200
(*Supplies large quantities only*)

Axminister Power Tools
Chard Street
Axminister
Hockley
Devon
EX13 5DZ
Tel: 01297 33656
(*Machinery and safety equipment*)

Bentley Chemicals Ltd
25 Church Road
Hoo Farm Industrial Est.
Kidderminster
Wocestershire

DY11 7RA
Tel: 01562 515 121
Fax: 01562 515 847
(*Supplies large quantities only*)

Canonbury Art Shop
266 Upper Street
London
N1 2UQ
Tel: 020 7226 4652
(*Jesmonite and non-toxic resin*)

Freeman Distribution Ltd
P.O. Box 8
5 Civic Way
Ellesmere Port
South Wirral
L65 0HB
Tel: 0151 356 3111
(*Supplies large quantitles only*)

Jacobsen Chemicals Ltd
Wylds Road
Churt, Nr Farnham
Surrey
GU10 2JD
Tel: 01428 713637

Llewellyn Ryland Ltd
Haden Street
Birmingham
B12 9DB
Tel: 0121 440 2284
Fax: 0121 440 0281
*(Suppliers of colours only)*

Merck Ltd
Merck House
Poole
BH15 1 TD
Tel: 01202 669 200
Fax: 01202 665599
*(Iridion powders (pearlescent))*

W.P. Notcutt Ltd
Rowland Way
Teddington
Middlesex
TW11 8PF
Tel: 020 8977 2252
Fax: 020 8977 6423
*(Supplies large quantities only)*

Scott Bader Company Ltd
Wollaston
Wellingborough
Northamtonshire
NN29 7RL
Tel: 01933 663 100
*(Supplies large quantities only)*
*This company also has regional centres in
Glasgow, West Midlands, Stockport,
Plymouth, Leeds, Cambridge and
Dublin*

Sterling Industrial Colours Ltd
14-18 High Street
London
E15 2QN

Tel: 020 8519 7711
*(Fluorescent colours for plastics)*

Alec Tiranti Ltd
70 High Street
Theale
Reading
RG7 5AR
Tel: 0118 930 2775
Fax: 0118 9323487

*also at*
27 Warren St
London
W1P 5DG

Trylon Ltd
Thrift Street
Wollaston
Northants
NN29 7QJ
Tel: 01933 664 275
Fax: 01933 664 960

Walsh
21 St Cross Street
Hatton Garden
London
EC1N 8UN
Tel: 020 7242 3711
Fax: 020 7242 3712

*also at*
1-2 Warstone Mews
Warstone Lane,
Birmingham
B18 6JB
*(Machinery and safety equipment)*

# US

Adtech Plastic Systems Corp
Charlotte
MI 48813–0532
http://www.adtechplastics.com
(*Distributes large quantities only*)

Ain Plastics
249 E. Stranford Blvd.
PO 151 Mt. Vernon
N.Y. 10550

Borden Chemical Inc
Louisville
KY 40202
(*Distributes large quantities only*)

CIBA Speciality Chemicals
Los Angeles
CA 90039
http://www.ciba-aero.com
(*Distributes large quantities only*)

Fiberclay
2425 NW Market St
Seattle
WA 98107
Tel: +1 800 942 0660
http://www.fiberclay.com
(*Resin, equipment, etc.*)

FRP Supply
Columbus
OH 43216
(*Distributes large quantities only*)

E. F. Fullam Incorporated
900 Albany Shaker Road
Latham

N.Y. 12110
Tel: +518 785 5533
Fax: +518 785 8647

GLS Corporation
833 Ridgeview Drive
McHenry
IL 60050
Tel: +815 385 8500
Fax: +815 385 8533
http://www.glscorporation.com

Industrial Plastics
309 Canal Street
New York City
N.Y. 10013

Nova Chemicals Incorporated
1550 Corapolis Heights Road
Pittsburgh
PA 15108
Tel: +412 490 4000
Fax: +412 490 4155

Pearl Paint
308 Canal Street
N.Y.C. 10013
(*Colours and mould materials*)

RBC Industries
80 Cypress Inc.
PO Box 8340
Warwick
RI 02888
http://www.rbcepoxy.com
Tel: +401 941 3000
Fax: +401 941 0150
(*Machinery and safety equipment*)

Reichhold
North American Composites Business
P.O. Box 13582
Research Triangle Park
NC 27709

Smooth-on
1000 Valley Road
Gillette
NJ 07933

Synairs
P.O. Box 5269
2003 Amnicola Highway
Chatanooga
TN 37406
Tel:  +423 697 0400
Fax: +423 697 0424

Zeon Chemicals
411 Bells
Louisville
KY 40211
Tel:  +502 775 2036
Fax: +502 775 2025

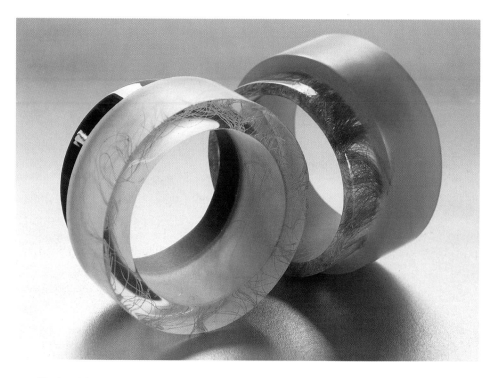

**Kathie Murphy**
Bangles, 2001.
Photo Norman Hollands.

# Bibliography

## Books

Arundell, Jan & Ted, *Design & Make – Polyester Jewellery*, (Dent, London), 1975. ISBN 0 4600 4121 5

Bussi, Buhs, *Kunstoff Als Kunstoff – Artificial Materials*, (Staatliche Akademie der Bildenden Künste, Munich, Germany), 1998. ISBN 3 9336 0202 5

Dormer & Turner, *The New Jewellery – Trends and Traditions*, (Thames & Hudson, UK), 1985.

Hollander, Harry B., *Plastics for Artists and Craftsmen*, Watson Guptill (New York), Pitman, (London), 1972. ISBN 0 2733 1801 2

Katz, Sylvia, *Classic Plastics*, (Thames & Hudson, UK), 1984. ISBN 0 500 2739 0

Meikle, Jeffrey, *American Plastic – A Cultural History*, (Rutgers University Press, New Jersey), 1995.

Quye, Anita, & Williamson, Colin, (Eds.), *Plastics – Collecting and Conserving*, (NMS Publishing Ltd), 1999. ISBN 1 9016 6312 4

Rees, David, *Creative Plastics*, (Studio Vista, London), 1973. ISBN 0 2897 0316 6

Scarfe, Herbert, *Introducing Resin Craft*, (Batsford, UK), 1973. ISBN 0 7134 24400

Untracht, Oppi, *Jewellery Concepts and Technology*, (Doubleday & Co. Inc), 1982. ISBN 0 3850 4185 3

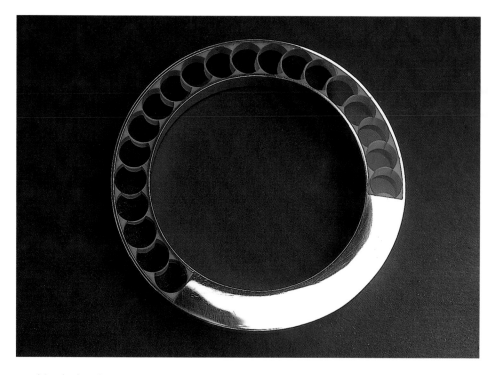

**Nuala Jamieson**
Bangle, silver, resin and acrylic, 1974.
Photo K.S. Murphy.

# Articles

Sandino, Linda, *Material Values*, Crafts Magazine, March/April, (The Crafts Council, UK), 2001.

*Avant Garde or Ashtray?* Schmuck Magazin, September 4, (Ebner Verlag Gmbh & Co. KG), 1999.

# Catalogues

Chang, Peter, *A Visionary*,(Taideteollisoumuseo, Finland). ISBN 952 9878 20 6

Heron & Ward, *The Jewellery Project*, (The Crafts Council, UK). ISBN 0 9037 9869 7

Katz, Sylvia, *Early Plastics*, (Shire Publications Ltd), 1986. ISBN 0 852 6379 0

# Index